# TIME TRAVELING TO 1965

## CELEBRATING A SPECIAL YEAR

TIME TRAVELING TO 1965

Author

Owen J. Wilder

Design

Gonçalo Sousa

November 2024

ISBN: 9798301237102

All Rights Reserved

© 2024 Owen J. Wilder

All the images of this book are reproduced under these permissions:

Owner's Permission

Creative Commons License

Fair Use Terms

Public Domain

All images are the property of their respective owners and are protected under international copyright laws.

## Surprise!

Dear reader, thank you so much for purchasing my book!

To make this book more (much more!) affordable, the images are all black & white, but I've created a special gift for you!

You can now have access, for FREE, to the PDF version of this book with the original images!

Keep in mind that some are originally black and white, but some are colored.

Go to page 101 and follow the instructions to download it.

I hope you enjoy it!

# Contents

## Chapter I: News & Current Events 1965

Leading Events — 9
Other Major Events — 14
Political Events — 18
Other Notable Events — 22

## Chapter II: Crime & Punishment 1965

Major Crime Events — 27

## Chapter III: Entertainment 1965

Silver Screen — 31
Top of the Charts — 42
Television — 47

## Chapter IV: Sports Review 1965

American Sports — 53
British Sports — 56
International Sports — 58

## Chapter V: General 1965

Pop Culture — 63
Technological Advancements — 67
Fashion — 70

| | |
|---|---|
| Cars | 74 |
| Popular Recreation | 77 |

## Chapter VI: Births & Deaths 1965

| | |
|---|---|
| Births | 85 |
| Deaths | 87 |

## Chapter VII: Statistics 1965 — 89

| | |
|---|---|
| Cost Of Things | 91 |

## Chapter VIII: Iconic Advertisements of 1965 — 93

# Chapter I: News & Current Events 1965

**Leading Events**

Selma to Montgomery March: Civil Rights Milestone - March 7

Harlem, NY, March 1965

The march from Selma to Montgomery became a pivotal moment in the struggle for civil rights, fueled by a desire for African Americans to secure their voting rights despite intense opposition. It began with about 600 protesters, including iconic leaders like Martin Luther King Jr., marching peacefully across the Edmund Pettus Bridge, only to be met with brutal violence by state troopers. This day, later known as "Bloody Sunday," sparked national outrage.

The horrific scenes, broadcast across the country, galvanized support for the civil rights movement. A second attempt to march ended in a strategic retreat, and during that time, activist James Reeb was tragically murdered.

Finally, under federal protection, thousands of marchers completed the 54-mile journey, arriving triumphantly in Montgomery, where they were joined by 25,000 demonstrators.

The national uproar surrounding the violence and persistence of the protesters led President Lyndon B. Johnson to address Congress in a historic televised speech, declaring, "We shall overcome." This momentum culminated in the passage of the Voting Rights Act, a monumental achievement in the fight against racial injustice, ensuring greater protection for African Americans to exercise their right to vote. The march's legacy endures, commemorated as a milestone in America's ongoing pursuit of equality.

### Malcolm X Assassinated: Civil Rights Leader Lost - February 21

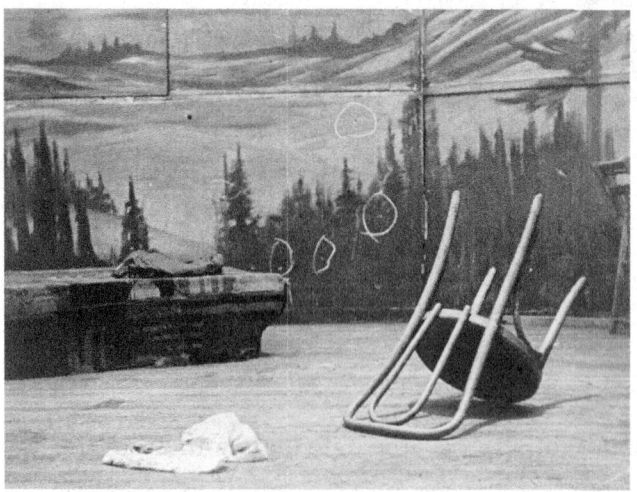

Bullet holes on stage where Malcolm X was shot

Malcolm X, a towering figure in the civil rights movement and a powerful advocate for Black empowerment, was tragically gunned down as he prepared to address a crowd at the Audubon Ballroom in New York. His life had been marked by bold speeches and fearless challenges to the status quo, particularly after breaking ties with the Nation of Islam. In the months leading up to his assassination, tensions between Malcolm X and the Nation grew, with death threats becoming frequent.

As he stood before his audience that day, a sudden disturbance was followed by gunshots. Malcolm X was struck by 21 bullets and pronounced dead shortly after arriving at the hospital. His murder sent shockwaves across the nation, fueling ongoing speculation about the involvement of the Nation of Islam and government agencies. Three men were convicted of the assassination, though two were exonerated decades later, leaving questions about who was truly responsible. Malcolm X's death, like the assassinations of other prominent leaders in the 1960s, became a grim reminder of the violent resistance to the fight for justice and equality. His legacy, however, endures as a symbol of resistance, defiance, and unyielding commitment to human rights.

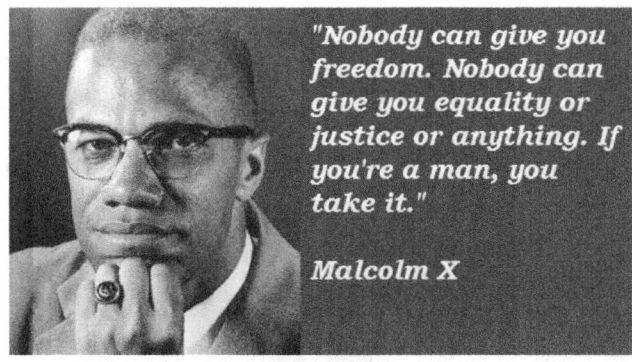

Malcolm X

## Medicare and Medicaid: Healthcare Milestones - July 30

In a monumental step for American healthcare, two groundbreaking programs—Medicare and Medicaid—were introduced, forever changing the landscape of medical coverage. Signed into law by President Lyndon B. Johnson as part of his ambitious Great Society agenda, these programs aimed to reduce poverty and provide essential healthcare to vulnerable populations. Johnson saw healthcare access as a fundamental right and believed these programs would protect millions from financial ruin due to medical expenses.

Johnson signs Medicare Bill with Truman, Independence, Mo.

Robert M. Ball presents on Medicare, 1965

Medicare provided health insurance to people 65 and older, as well as younger individuals with disabilities, offering protection against skyrocketing hospital and outpatient costs. With different parts addressing everything from hospital stays to prescription drugs, Medicare became a crucial safety net for millions of seniors and those battling chronic diseases. Medicaid, managed by both state and federal governments, helped low-income individuals and families access healthcare they couldn't afford otherwise. It also became a lifeline for nursing home care and long-term support, providing essential services for the elderly and disabled.

These programs not only helped millions avoid medical debt, but also established a foundation of healthcare rights in the U.S., reshaping public health and ensuring access for nearly one-third of the population today.

**First U.S. Combat Troops Arrive in Vietnam - March 8**

As the U.S. escalated its involvement in Vietnam, the arrival of American combat troops marked a turning point in the conflict. What began as a limited advisory role evolved into full-scale military intervention, driven by Cold War fears of communist expansion in Southeast Asia. Under the pressure of the "Domino Theory," the U.S. believed that if Vietnam fell to communism, neighboring countries would follow. This geopolitical strategy framed Vietnam not just as a regional battle, but as a critical front in the global struggle against communism.

President Lyndon B. Johnson, inheriting a complex situation from his predecessor, John F. Kennedy, faced the difficult decision of either pulling back or committing fully to military action. His reluctance to appear soft on communism, combined with domestic political concerns, pushed him to send combat troops. However, the conflict quickly spiraled into a costly and prolonged war that would eventually claim tens of thousands of American lives.

First U.S. combat troops arrive in Vietnam via beach landing

The arrival of U.S. troops was the start of a massive military buildup, which peaked in the late 1960s. Despite efforts to contain communism, the war became increasingly unpopular, with growing opposition back home. The Vietnam War's legacy continues to shape U.S. foreign policy, leaving deep scars on the American psyche.

**Pope Paul VI Makes Historic US Visit - October 4**

Pope Paul VI made history with his whirlwind 14-hour visit to New York City, marking the first time a pope had ever set foot in the United States. The visit was packed with significant moments, starting with a blessing at St. Patrick's Cathedral, where thousands gathered to see the pontiff. He then met with President Lyndon B. Johnson before addressing the United Nations, delivering a powerful message of peace and diplomacy to world leaders.

Continuing his fast-paced day, the pope celebrated a public mass at Yankee Stadium, drawing a crowd of over 90,000 faithful. The spectacle was emblematic of his mission to bridge the church and the modern world. He even found time to visit the World's Fair in Queens, where he viewed

# 1965

Michelangelo's Pieta. Pope Paul VI's visit was a groundbreaking moment not just for the Catholic Church, but for global diplomacy and interfaith relations. Known as "the Pilgrim Pope," his travels opened new doors for future pontiffs, making international outreach a key aspect of the papacy.

Pope Paul VI celebrated the first pontifical Mass on U.S. soil at the Yankee Stadium

This momentous visit remains a landmark in the history of both the Catholic Church and the United States, symbolizing a growing connection between faith and world affairs.

## Other Major Events

### Cosmonaut Alexei Leonov Performs First Spacewalk - March 18

The first spacewalk by Alexei Leonov

Alexei Leonov made history as the first human to step into the void of space, floating outside his Voskhod 2 spacecraft. For just over 12 minutes, Leonov was tethered to his capsule, showcasing the Soviet Union's space ambitions in its race with the U.S. However, his pioneering spacewalk wasn't without peril.

While floating in the vacuum of space, Leonov's suit ballooned, making it impossible for him to re-enter the airlock. In a daring and risky move, he released air from his suit, pushing it beyond safe limits. As a result, he suffered from decompression sickness, with sweat accumulating inside his suit.

Despite these harrowing moments, Leonov's spacewalk was a monumental achievement, marking a bold step in human space exploration and setting the stage for future missions, including humanity's eventual walk on the moon. His courage under pressure remains a testament to human ingenuity and resilience.

## Blackout in Northeast: Millions Affected - November 9

The Northeast blackout plunged over 30 million people across parts of the U.S. and Canada into darkness for up to 13 hours. The power failure, triggered by a relay issue at a plant near Niagara Falls, caused a domino effect that left 80,000 square miles without electricity. Major cities, including New York, experienced the blackout, with Manhattan and much of the surrounding area going dark just after 5:30 p.m.

Despite the chaos, the night saw remarkably low crime rates, with only a handful of looting incidents reported. Many subway passengers were stranded, and some hospitals had to operate by flashlight. A full moon provided a bit of natural

Front page of the Telegram on November 10, 1965

light, helping people navigate the powerless streets. Power restoration took hours, with some areas not seeing light until the next morning.

The event sparked significant upgrades to power grid monitoring, and in the aftermath, even inspired an R&B song, "New York in the Dark," celebrating the city's resilience during the unexpected blackout.

## India-Pakistan War over Kashmir - September 6

The Indo-Pakistani War erupted over the contested region of Kashmir, following Pakistan's failed Operation Gibraltar, which sought to incite an insurgency against Indian rule. Over the next few weeks, the two nations engaged in fierce battles, leading to one of the largest tank engagements since World War II. Both sides suffered heavy casualties, with intense fighting occurring on land and in the air.

Although India gained a slight advantage by the time a ceasefire was declared, neither side achieved a decisive victory. International pressure from the United Nations, along with diplomatic intervention by the Soviet Union and the United States, led to the signing of the Tashkent Declaration, ending hostilities.

The conflict left a lasting impact on both nations' foreign relations, as distrust towards the Western powers grew due to their perceived lack of support. This marked a significant shift in the geopolitical landscape of the subcontinent, with India and Pakistan aligning more closely with the Soviet Union and China, respectively.

Indian soldiers with a destroyed Pakistani M4A1 Sherman tank

## Mariner 4 Sends First Mars Photos - July 14

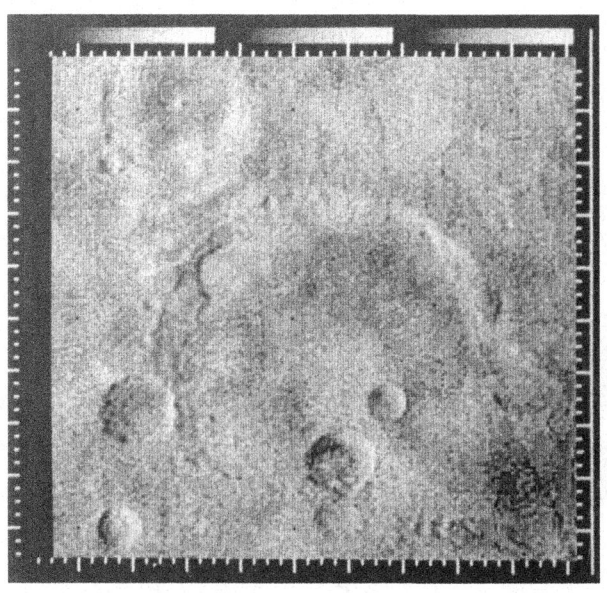

Image of Mars captured by the Mariner 4 space probe

Mariner 4 made history by sending the first close-up images of Mars, changing our understanding of the Red Planet forever. Launched as part of NASA's early efforts in planetary exploration, Mariner 4's flyby mission revealed a cold, cratered world that was far from the life-supporting planet many had imagined. These images, the first ever sent back from deep space, showed a barren, Moon-like surface, challenging scientists' views on the potential for life on Mars.

Despite technical hurdles - such as using a spare tape recorder and hand-coloring pixel data to verify the camera's function - the mission was a success. Mariner 4 gathered critical data, including atmospheric pressure and surface temperatures, while confirming the absence of surface water and magnetic fields.

The mission's findings, although surprising, laid the groundwork for future Mars exploration, giving humanity its first glimpse of another planet. Mariner 4's legacy lives on as a pioneering step in interplanetary exploration, reshaping our expectations of Mars and the solar system.

## Griswold v. Connecticut: Contraceptive Rights Case - June 7

The U.S. Supreme Court's decision in Griswold v. Connecticut was a pivotal moment in the fight for privacy and reproductive rights. The case challenged a Connecticut law that made it illegal for married couples to

Dr. C. Lee Buxton (center) and Mrs. Estelle Griswold (right) at police headquarters, after their arrest

use contraceptives. Estelle Griswold, head of Planned Parenthood in Connecticut, and Dr. C. Lee Buxton, a gynecologist, opened a birth control clinic to test the law, ultimately leading to their arrest.

In a 7-2 ruling, the Court struck down the law, establishing a constitutional "right to marital privacy."

Justice William O. Douglas, writing for the majority, argued that various amendments created "penumbras" or zones of privacy that shielded personal decisions from government interference. The ruling was a major victory for reproductive rights and laid the groundwork for future cases concerning privacy and bodily autonomy, including later rulings on abortion and contraception. The decision affirmed that deeply personal choices within marriage were beyond the reach of the state.

## Political Events

### Voting Rights Act Signed into Law - August 6

Johnson meets King at Voting Rights Act signing, 1965

The Voting Rights Act was a transformative piece of legislation signed into law during the height of the civil rights movement. It aimed to eliminate racial discrimination in voting, particularly in the South, where practices like literacy tests and poll taxes disenfranchised Black voters. The Act enforced the rights guaranteed by the Fourteenth and Fifteenth Amendments, marking a significant victory in the fight for equality.

A key provision of the Act, Section 5, required certain states with a history of discriminatory practices to obtain federal approval before changing their voting laws. The law led to a dramatic increase in voter registration among racial minorities and reshaped American politics by empowering millions of disenfranchised citizens. Though later rulings weakened some protections, the Voting Rights Act remains a cornerstone of civil rights legislation in the U.S., credited with safeguarding the democratic process.

Johnson signs Voting Rights Act as Martin Luther King Jr. looks on

## Singapore Independence: New Nation Born - August 9

Singapore's unexpected independence was born out of turmoil when it was expelled from Malaysia after a brief and tense union. Struggling with racial tensions, political disagreements, and economic disparities, the relationship between Singapore and the federal government in Kuala Lumpur deteriorated. Prime Minister Lee Kuan Yew's push for equality among all races clashed with Malaysia's policies favoring Malays, leading to unrest and eventually a complete breakdown in relations.

# 1965

Singapore's first national day parade

On the day of the separation, Lee Kuan Yew tearfully announced Singapore's new status as an independent nation. Despite its lack of resources and facing numerous challenges like unemployment and housing shortages, Singapore, under Lee's leadership, transformed itself into a global economic powerhouse. This small island nation defied expectations, evolving from a third-world country to a first-world success story by the end of the century.

## Rhodesian Unilateral Declaration of Independence - November 11

Rhodesia's Unilateral Declaration of Independence (UDI) marked a historic and controversial moment when the white-minority government of Prime Minister Ian Smith declared the territory an independent state, breaking from British rule. The UDI came after protracted disputes with Britain over decolonization, with the UK insisting that Rhodesia could

Signing the unilateral declaration of independence

not gain independence without majority (black) rule. Smith's government, representing just 5% of the population, refused, believing they were entitled to independence after decades of self-governance.

The declaration was condemned globally, with the UK, Commonwealth, and United Nations imposing sanctions. Despite this, Rhodesia maintained its unrecognized status, relying on support from South Africa and Portugal. The UDI eventually led to a prolonged guerrilla war, and in 1979, Rhodesia returned to British control, paving the way for recognized independence under black-majority rule as Zimbabwe in 1980.

## Dominican Civil War: US Intervention - April 28

US troops patrol the streets near a food line in Santo Domingo

The Dominican Civil War erupted when supporters of ousted President Juan Bosch overthrew the military-installed leader, Donald Reid Cabral. The conflict quickly escalated into a struggle between "constitutionalist" rebels and loyalist military forces. Fearing communist influence within the rebel ranks, the United States intervened, launching Operation Power Pack, deploying thousands of troops to the Dominican Republic.

Though officially neutral, U.S. forces largely supported the anti-Bosch faction. Tensions peaked in June during fierce fighting between U.S. paratroopers and Dominican forces, resulting in hundreds of casualties. By September, international peacekeepers from the Organization of American

States replaced U.S. troops, stabilizing the situation. In 1966, elections were held, with Joaquín Balaguer winning the presidency, ending the conflict that left around 6,000 Dominicans and 350 U.S. soldiers dead or wounded.

## Other Notable Events

### Gateway Arch Completed in St. Louis - October 28

The placing of the last link in the Gateway Arch, 1965, St. Louis, Mo.

Standing 630 feet tall, the Gateway Arch in St. Louis is the world's tallest arch and a symbol of westward expansion in the U.S. Designed by Finnish-American architect Eero Saarinen, the Arch was envisioned as a tribute to pioneers and built to revive the St. Louis riverfront. Construction began in 1963, and despite financial concerns and opposition from locals, the sleek stainless-steel structure was completed two years later. Costing $13 million at the time, the project was funded with federal support and aimed to create jobs during a time of economic hardship. Today, the Gateway Arch is a celebrated monument, drawing millions of visitors and standing as a reminder of America's adventurous spirit.

### First American Spacewalk: Ed White - June 3

Ed White made history as the first American to walk in space during the Gemini 4 mission. As he floated outside the spacecraft, tethered by a 25-foot cord, White marveled at the breathtaking view of Earth below, describing the experience as the "most exhilarating" moment of his life. His spacewalk lasted 23 minutes, during which he used a handheld maneuvering gun to control his movement. White's feat marked a major milestone for NASA, demonstrating the capability of astronauts to work outside spacecraft - a critical step toward future lunar missions. His pioneering spirit and

A photograph of Ed White taken by Commander James McDivitt over a cloud-covered Pacific Ocean

bravery earned him widespread acclaim and posthumous honors following his untimely death in the Apollo 1 tragedy.

Gemini Titan III lifts off Launch Pad 19

### Gemini 3: First Manned Mission - March 23

Gemini 3 marked a major milestone as NASA's first crewed Gemini mission, piloted by astronauts Gus Grissom and John Young. Their spacecraft, nicknamed Molly Brown, completed three orbits of Earth, testing the Gemini program's maneuverability by firing thrusters to change orbit shape and altitude. This was a crucial step in preparing for future lunar missions. Gemini 3 also demonstrated improved re-entry control, allowing the spacecraft to adjust its landing point, a first for U.S. missions. The flight achieved several key objectives and was the final manned mission controlled from Cape Kennedy, before mission control moved to Houston.

## The Grateful Dead's First Concert - December 10

The Grateful Dead's first concert

The Grateful Dead's first concert marked the birth of a band that would become legendary for its unique blend of rock, blues, jazz, and psychedelic improvisation. Formed in the San Francisco Bay Area during the rise of the 1960s counterculture, the group—featuring Jerry Garcia, Bob Weir, Phil Lesh, Ron "Pigpen" McKernan, and Bill Kreutzmann—quickly gained a devoted following known as "Deadheads." Originally named the Warlocks, the band changed its name to the Grateful Dead and pioneered the "jam band" genre, known for long, improvised live performances. Though they had only one Top-40 hit, their music became a cultural touchstone, earning them a lasting legacy and induction into the Rock and Roll Hall of Fame.

# First Commercial Satellite (Intelsat I) Launched - April 6

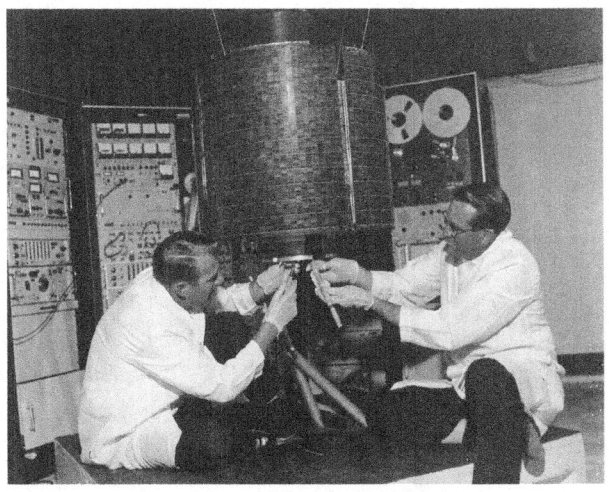

Engineers Stanley Peterson and Ray Bowerman check the "Early Bird", first communication satellite

Intelsat I, also known as "Early Bird," was the first commercial communications satellite launched into geosynchronous orbit. This groundbreaking satellite revolutionized global communication by enabling direct, near-instantaneous contact between Europe and North America. It transmitted television, telephone, and fax signals, providing the first live TV coverage of events like the Gemini 6 splashdown. Though designed to operate for only 18 months, Early Bird remained active for over four years. Incredibly, it was even reactivated during the Apollo 11 mission to ensure coverage. Early Bird set the stage for modern global communication networks, leaving an indelible mark on space history.

# Chapter II: Crime & Punishment 1965

## Major Crime Events

### Watts Riots: Six Days of Unrest in LA - August 11-16

Aerial view of buildings on fire on Avalon Blvd during Watts Riots

The Watts Riots, also known as the Watts Uprising, erupted in Los Angeles following the arrest of 21-year-old Marquette Frye, a Black man accused of drunk driving. Tensions escalated when a scuffle broke out between Frye, his family, and police, sparking rumors that a pregnant woman had been assaulted by officers. This incident ignited six days of unrest fueled by deep-seated anger over police brutality, racial discrimination, and economic inequalities faced by the African-American community in L.A. The riots resulted in 34 deaths, over 1,000 injuries, and $40 million in property damage. Nearly 14,000 National Guardsmen were deployed to restore order. The McCone Commission later attributed the riots to high unemployment, poor education, and substandard living conditions, though many of its recommended reforms were never enacted.

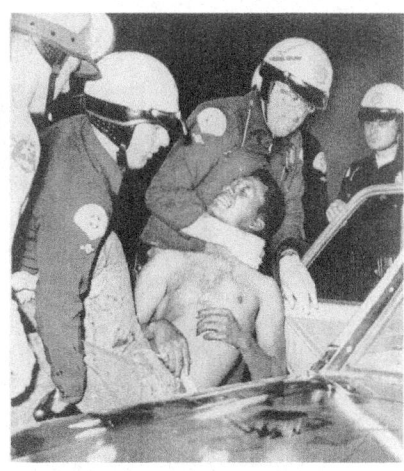

Police arrests a man during the riots on August 12

## Moors Murders: Infamous Killing Spree Ends - October 1965

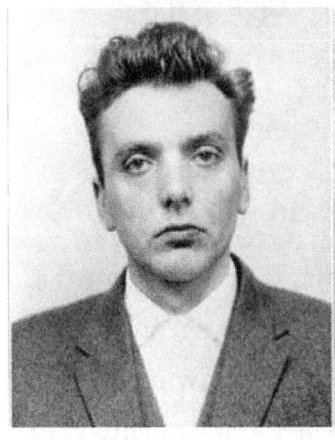
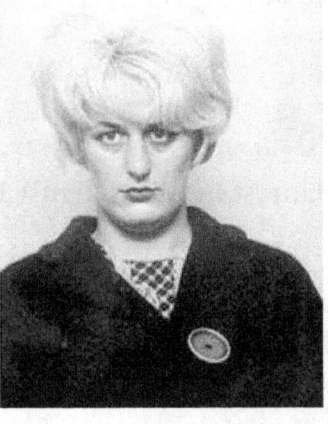

Brady and Hindley after their arrests

The Moors Murders, one of the most notorious criminal cases in British history, came to a grim end with the arrest of Ian Brady and Myra Hindley. Between 1963 and 1965, the pair abducted and killed five children in the Manchester area, burying several of their victims on Saddleworth Moor. Their crimes were uncovered after the murder of 17-year-old Edward Evans, which was witnessed by Hindley's brother-in-law, David Smith, who reported it to the police. Investigators found disturbing evidence, including photos and audio recordings, that tied the couple to the brutal killings. Both Brady and Hindley were convicted and sentenced to life imprisonment, leaving a lasting scar on the nation and a legacy of horror that still resonates today.

## Hickock and Smith Executed for Clutter Family Murders - April 14

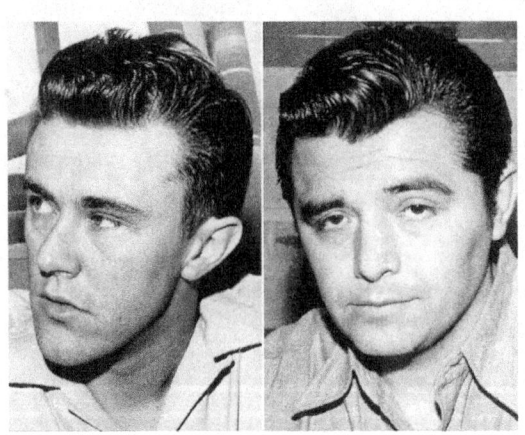

Perry Smith and Richard Hickock

The Clutter family murders, detailed in Truman Capote's "In Cold Blood", were among the most infamous killings of the time. In 1959, ex-convicts Perry Smith and Richard Hickock brutally murdered Herb Clutter, his wife Bonnie, and their two teenage children, Nancy and

Kenyon, in their Kansas farmhouse. The two men, believing the family had a hidden fortune, found no money but left behind a devastating crime scene. Captured six weeks later, Smith and Hickock were convicted and sentenced to death. Their execution

The Clutter family

marked the end of this tragic case, which shocked the nation and became a seminal moment in true crime history, solidified by Capote's masterful narrative.

## Court Supports Selma Marchers' Rights - March 16

Civil rights march from Selma to Montgomery, Alabama

On March 16, a federal court ruled in favor of civil rights activists in Selma, Alabama, affirming their right to march from Selma to Montgomery. This decision came after a series of violent clashes, most notably on "Bloody

# 1965

Sunday" when peaceful demonstrators were brutally attacked by state troopers on the Edmund Pettus Bridge. The marchers were advocating for voting rights, a critical issue for African Americans facing significant barriers to voter registration.

The ruling allowed the protesters, led by Martin Luther King Jr., to proceed under federal protection, with thousands joining the historic march. This pivotal moment galvanized national attention, culminating in the passage of the Voting Rights Act later that year.

# Chapter III: Entertainment 1965

## Silver Screen

### Top Film of 1965: The Sound of Music

The Sound of Music

"The Sound of Music," directed by Robert Wise and released in 1965, became an instant box-office success, eventually surpassing "Gone with the Wind" as the highest-grossing film of all time. Based on the 1949 memoir by Maria von Trapp, the film follows the story of Maria (Julie Andrews), a governess to the seven von Trapp children, and her romance with their father, Captain Georg von Trapp (Christopher Plummer), set against the backdrop of the Nazi Anschluss in Austria.

Featuring iconic songs by Rodgers and Hammerstein, such as "Do-Re-Mi" and "My Favorite Things," the film combined breathtaking scenery of Salzburg with heartfelt performances. While initial critical response was mixed, audiences flocked to see the film, making it the top-grossing picture of 1965. It won five Academy Awards, including Best Picture and Best Director, and was hailed for its universal appeal, eventually grossing $286 million worldwide.

The film's cultural impact endures, with "The Sound of Music" regularly featured on best film lists and preserved in the U.S. National Film Registry for its historical significance. Despite early skepticism, it has become a beloved cinematic classic, known for its heartwarming story, memorable music, and timeless charm.

## Remaining Top 3

Doctor Zhivago

### Doctor Zhivago

"Doctor Zhivago," directed by David Lean and released in 1965, is an epic historical romance set during World War I and the Russian Revolution. Starring Omar Sharif as Yuri Zhivago and Julie Christie as Lara Antipova, the film follows the tragic love story between the married physician-poet and his muse, set against the sweeping backdrop of political upheaval in Russia.

Though criticized for its romanticization of the revolution, the film captivated audiences with its lush cinematography and Maurice Jarre's iconic score, including "Lara's Theme." Despite a runtime of over three hours, it became the second highest-grossing film of 1965 and remains one of the highest-grossing films of all time, adjusted for inflation.

"Doctor Zhivago" won five Academy Awards, including Best Adapted Screenplay and Best Cinematography. Its grand scale, coupled with Lean's expert direction, has cemented it as a classic, often hailed for its visual splendor and emotional depth.

## Thunderball

Thunderball

"Thunderball" (1965), the fourth James Bond film, stars Sean Connery as the iconic MI6 agent in a mission to recover two stolen NATO atomic bombs. Directed by Terence Young, the film is an adaptation of Ian Fleming's novel and features Bond battling the villainous SPECTRE operative Emilio Largo in the Bahamas.

Known for its spectacular underwater sequences, "Thunderball" was the first Bond film shot in widescreen Panavision and ran over two hours. Its thrilling underwater battle and Connery's charm made it a box-office hit, grossing $141.2 million worldwide and making it the most financially successful Bond film at the time.

Despite some criticism for its length and pacing, "Thunderball" won the Academy Award for Best Visual Effects and remains a fan favorite for its action-packed plot and luxurious settings. The film helped solidify the Bond franchise's global appeal and is still considered one of the most successful entries in the series.

 Top 1965 Movies at The Domestic Box Office (thenumbers.com)

| Rank | Title | Release Date | 1965 Gross |
|---|---|---|---|
| 1 | The Sound of Music | Mar 2, 1965 | $163,214,286 |
| 2 | Doctor Zhivago | Dec 22, 1965 | $111,721,913 |
| 3 | Thunderball | Dec 29, 1965 | $63,600,000 |
| 4 | Those Magnificent Men in Their Flying Machines | Jun 16, 1965 | $31,111,111 |
| 5 | That Darn Cat! | Dec 2, 1965 | $28,062,222 |
| 6 | The Great Race | Jul 1, 1965 | $25,333,333 |
| 7 | Cat Ballou | Jun 24, 1965 | $20,666,667 |
| 8 | What's New, Pussycat | Jun 22, 1965 | $18,820,000 |
| 9 | Shenandoah | Jun 3, 1965 | $17,268,889 |
| 10 | Von Ryan's Express | Jun 23, 1965 | $17,111,111 |

## Other Film Releases

In 1965, a diverse collection of films emerged that initially flew under the radar but later developed cult followings, capturing the imaginations of niche audiences. These six cult classics—"Faster, Pussycat! Kill! Kill!", "Repulsion", "The Tenth Victim", "The Hill", "Planet of the Vampires", and "Chimes at Midnight"—pushed cinematic boundaries and have since been celebrated for their unique contributions to the art of filmmaking.

Leading this group is Russ Meyer's "Faster, Pussycat! Kill! Kill!", a provocative exploitation film that combined fast cars, deadly women, and intense action. Despite its initial reception as low-budget pulp, it has since become a feminist cult icon. The film follows three go-go dancers who wreak havoc in the desert, portraying fierce women who defy societal expectations and take control. Its over-the-top violence and energetic style have made it a staple at midnight movie screenings, where its influence continues to inspire filmmakers and fans alike.

Roman Polanski's "Repulsion" represents one of the most disturbing and powerful depictions of psychological horror. This unsettling masterpiece follows Carol (Catherine Deneuve), a woman whose isolation leads to a terrifying breakdown. With Polanski's masterful direction and chilling cinematography, "Repulsion" explores themes of fear, repression, and mental illness. It was initially overshadowed by larger films, but its influence has grown, making it one of the most significant psychological thrillers of its era.

Faster, Pussycat! Kill! Kill!

Repulsion

# 1965

The Tenth Victim

The Hill

"The Tenth Victim", an Italian sci-fi thriller directed by Elio Petri, presents a futuristic society obsessed with televised violence. The film blends satirical commentary with stylish, mod visuals, making it a forerunner to many dystopian narratives. Although it didn't achieve immediate international success, its unique take on media manipulation and violence found resonance with audiences in later years, earning it a cult following among sci-fi fans.

Sidney Lumet's "The Hill", a harrowing war drama starring Sean Connery, was not a commercial hit, but its intense portrayal of military punishment and power struggles has made it a favorite among fans of serious, thought-provoking cinema. The film's unrelenting atmosphere and Connery's powerful performance elevated its status over time.

Mario Bava's "Planet of the Vampires" became a cult classic through its atmospheric set design and innovative approach to horror and sci-fi. Its chilling visual aesthetic and influence on later genre films like "Alien" secured its place in cult film history.

Planet of the Vampires

Chimes at Midnight

Lastly, Orson Welles' "Chimes at Midnight", based on Shakespeare's history plays, was critically acclaimed but overlooked upon release. Over time, it has gained recognition for Welles' compelling performance as Falstaff and its groundbreaking cinematic techniques, solidifying its status as one of Welles' finest achievements.

Each of these films contributed to the evolution of cult cinema by exploring unique themes and experimental styles, resonating with audiences long after their initial releases.

# The 22nd Golden Globe Awards – Monday, February 8th, 1965

🏆 Winners

Best Motion Picture – Drama: Becket

Best Motion Picture – Comedy or Musical: My Fair Lady

Best Performance in a Motion Picture – Drama – Actor:
Peter O'Toole (Becket)

Best Performance in a Motion Picture – Drama - Actress:
Anne Bancroft (The Pumpkin Eater)

1965

Best Performance in a Motion Picture – Comedy or Musical – Actor: Rex Harrison (My Fair Lady)

Best Performance in a Motion Picture – Comedy or Musical – Actress: Julie Andrews (Mary Poppins)

Best Supporting Performance in a Motion Picture – Drama, Comedy or Musical – Actor: Edmond O'Brien (Seven Days in May)

Best Supporting Performance in a Motion Picture – Drama, Comedy or Musical – Actress: Agnes Moorehead (Hush...Hush, Sweet Charlotte)

Best Director: George Cukor (My Fair Lady)

# The 18th British Academy Film Awards – 1965

## 🏆 Winners

Best British Actor:
Richard Attenborough (Guns at Batasi)

Best British Actress:
Audrey Hepburn (Charade)

Best Foreign Actor: Marcello Mastroianni
(Yesterday, Today and Tomorrow)

Best Foreign Actress:
Anne Bancroft (The Pumpkin Eater)

Best British Screenplay:
Harold Pinter (The Pumpkin Eater)

Best Film & Best British Film:
Dr. Strangelove (Stanley Kubrick)

1965

# The 37th Academy Awards – Monday, April 5th, 1965 – Santa Monica Civic Auditorium, Santa Monica, California

🏆 Winners

Best Actor in a Leading Role:
Rex Harrison (My Fair Lady)

Best Actress in a Leading Role:
Julie Andrews (Mary Poppins)

Best Supporting Actor:
Peter Ustinov (Topkapi)

Best Supporting Actress:
Lila Kedrova (Zorba the Greek)

Best Cinematography (Black-and-White):
Walter Lassally (Zorba the Greek)

Best Cinematography (Color):
Harry Stradling (My Fair Lady)

41

# 1965

Best Song: Richard M. Sherman and Robert B. Sherman ("Chim Chim Cher-ee" from Mary Poppins)

Best Director: George Cukor (My Fair Lady)

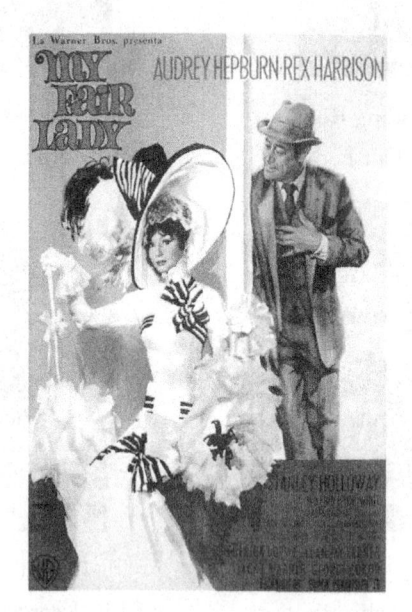

Best Picture: My Fair Lady (Jack L. Warner)

## Top of the Charts

Top Album: "Rubber Soul" by The Beatles

Released on December 3, 1965, "Rubber Soul," the Beatles' sixth studio album, marked a pivotal artistic shift. The album saw the band skillfully blending folk rock, soul, and pop influences, drawing inspiration from Bob Dylan, Motown, and emerging counterculture. With introspective lyrics and a range of emotions, it captured the band's newfound sophistication and emotional depth. New instrumentation, like sitar and fuzz bass, showcased their evolving creativity and openness to global sounds. The album was both a critical and commercial success, cementing the Beatles' status as musical innovators and advancing the concept of the album as an art form. "Rubber Soul" also influenced iconic artists like Brian Wilson, fueling a transformative era in music.

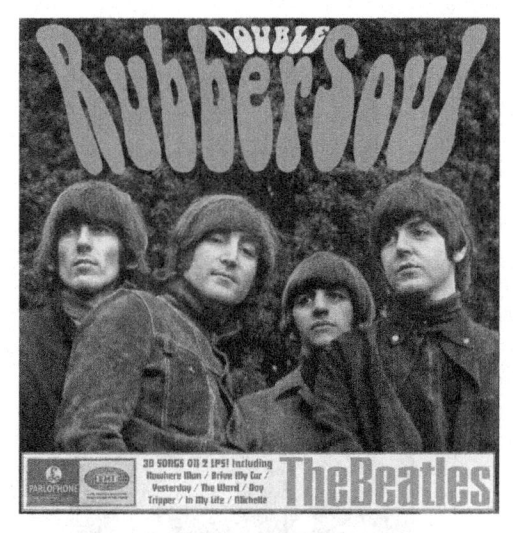

Rubber Soul

## Best Albums and Singles

In 1965, music showcased a delightful blend of Broadway, folk, and emerging pop sounds. "The Sound of Music" by Richard Rodgers captured hearts with its timeless melodies, while Disney's "Mary Poppins" delighted listeners with whimsical tunes. Bob Dylan's "Highway 61 Revisited" and "Bringing It All Back Home" brought a new edge to folk, reflecting Dylan's shift toward

The Sound of Music

Mary Poppins

electric sounds. Herb Alpert's "Whipped Cream & Other Delights" added playful jazz, and "Help!" by The Beatles showcased their evolving musical style.

Highway 61 Revisited

Bringing It All Back Home

Whipped Cream & Other Delights

Help!

On the singles chart, Sam The Sham and The Pharaohs' "Wooly Bully" brought fun and rhythm, while the Four Tops' "I Can't Help Myself" radiated soulful energy.

The Rolling Stones' "(I Can't Get No) Satisfaction" became an anthem of rebellion, and We Five's "You Were On My Mind" offered a folk-pop touch. Music in 1965 balanced tradition and innovation beautifully.

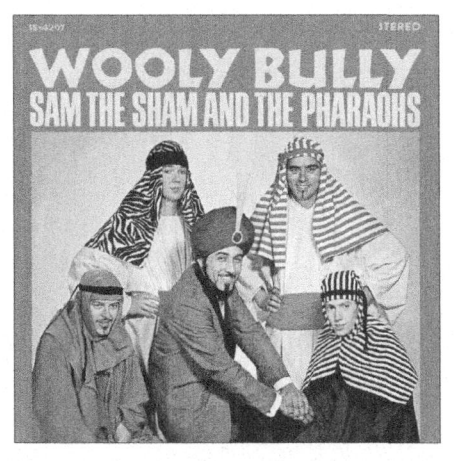

Wooly Bully

I Can't Help Myself

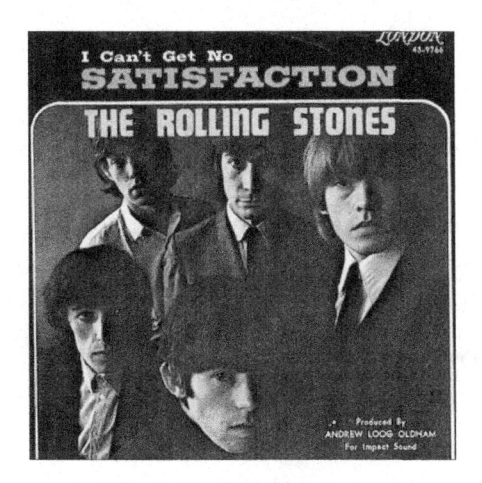

(I Can't Get No) Satisfaction

You Were On My Mind

🎵 Top Albums 1965 (tsort.info):

1. The Beatles - Rubber Soul
2. Richard Rodgers - The Sound Of Music
3. The Beatles - Help!
4. Bob Dylan - Highway 61 Revisited
5. Bob Dylan - Bringing It All Back Home
6. Disney - Mary Poppins
7. Herb Alpert - Whipped Cream & Other Delights
8. The Beatles - Beatles For Sale

9. The Rolling Stones - Out Of Our Heads
10. Original Cast – Fiddler On The Roof

## ♪ Top Singles 1965 (billboardtop100of.com):

1. Sam The Sham and The Pharaohs - Wooly Bully
2. Four Tops - I Can't Help Myself (Sugar Pie Honey Bunch)
3. Rolling Stones - (I Can't Get No) Satisfaction
4. We Five - You Were On My Mind
5. Righteous Brothers - You've Lost That Lovin' Feelin'
6. Petula Clark - Downtown
7. Beatles - Help!
8. Herman's Hermits - Can't You Hear My Heartbeat
9. Elvis Presley - Crying In The Chapel
10. Temptations - My Girl

## The 7th Annual Grammy Awards – Tuesday, April 13th, 1965 – Beverly Hilton Hotel, Beverly Hills

🏆 Winners

Record of the Year: Astrud Gilberto & Stan Getz for "The Girl from Ipanema"

Album of the Year: "Getz/Gilberto" – João Gilberto & Stan Getz

Song of the Year: "Hello, Dolly!" – Jerry Herman (songwriter), performed by Louis Armstrong

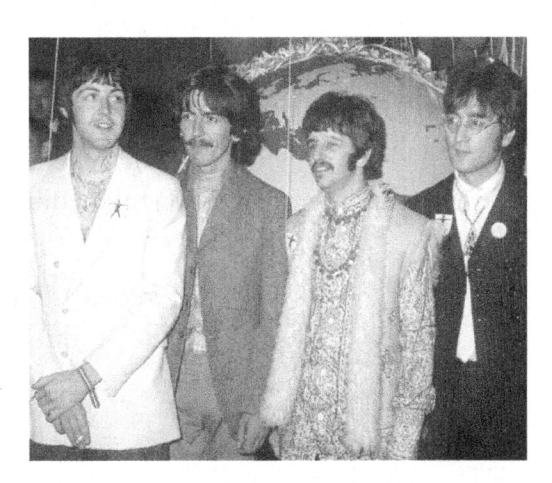

Best New Artist: The Beatles

## Television

In 1965, television was rapidly expanding its influence, offering a variety of shows that shaped the viewing habits of audiences across the UK and the US. In the UK, viewers had the option of BBC and ITV, with popular programs like "Public Eye" and "Jackanory" capturing attention. Meanwhile, the

Public Eye

Lost in Space

# 1965

US had three dominant networks: ABC, CBS, and NBC, each rolling out groundbreaking shows such as "Lost in Space" and "The Wild Wild West". This era reflected the growing cultural significance of TV, as it became a household staple and a powerful medium for entertainment and news.

**"I Spy" Premieres: Bill Cosby Makes History - September 15**

The TV series "I Spy" made history with its premiere, introducing Bill Cosby as one of the first Black actors in a lead role on American television. Partnered with Robert Culp, the duo portrayed U.S. secret agents navigating international espionage, disguised as tennis players. Notably, Cosby's race was never the focus of the show, a groundbreaking decision for the time. The on-screen chemistry between Cosby and Culp, paired with filming in exotic global locations, made "I Spy" a trailblazer, influencing the future of spy dramas and buddy television series.

I Spy

**"A Charlie Brown Christmas" Debuts on CBS - December 9**

"A Charlie Brown Christmas" made its television debut, introducing the Peanuts gang to TV audiences in a heartwarming holiday special. It defied expectations, with its unconventional jazz soundtrack, use of child voice actors, and lack of a laugh track. Charlie Brown's quest to find the true meaning of Christmas resonated

A Charlie Brown Christmas

with viewers, particularly through Linus' famous reading of the Nativity story. Despite network skepticism, it became an instant classic, earning critical acclaim and paving the way for future Peanuts specials. Its message of simplicity and sincerity continues to touch audiences today.

## "The Beatles Cartoon Show" Premieres on ABC - September 25

"The Beatles Cartoon Show" premiered to great fanfare, offering animated adventures of the Fab Four with episodes based on their hit songs. Despite initial skepticism from the band members about its quality, the show quickly became a ratings success. Audiences enjoyed its colorful animation, light-hearted storytelling, and playful incorporation of Beatles music.

Featuring exaggerated character designs and voiced by professional actors, the series aired for three seasons and introduced the band to a younger generation. Over time, even the Beatles grew to appreciate the show's quirky charm.

The Beatles Cartoon Show

## First NFL Game Broadcast in Color on CBS - November 25

On Thanksgiving Day, CBS made television history by airing the first NFL game in color. The game featured the traditional matchup at Detroit, giving fans across the country a vivid, enhanced viewing experience. This

# 1965

color broadcast marked a significant shift in sports media, as CBS had only recently begun using their color mobile unit. Although only a handful of games were broadcast in color that season, the move paved the way for all NFL telecasts to be shown in color just a few years later, revolutionizing how fans experienced the sport.

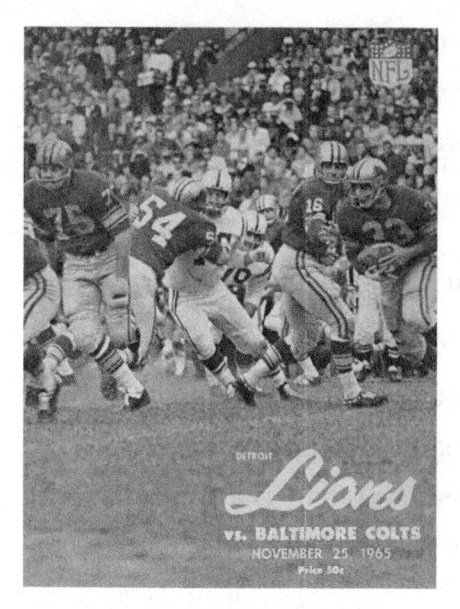

First color NFL broadcast airs on CBS: Detroit Lions vs. Baltimore Colts

## "Days of Our Lives" Premieres - November 8

When "Days of Our Lives" premiered, it introduced viewers to the fictional town of Salem, setting the stage for decades of drama centered around the Horton and Brady families. This soap opera became a staple of daytime television, exploring family life, love, and emotional turmoil. Created by Ted and Betty Corday, the show was groundbreaking, addressing controversial themes such as mental health and love across class lines. The series quickly gained a loyal following, evolving into one of the longest-running television programs, and remains beloved by fans to this day.

Days of Our Lives

## Julie Andrews' First TV Special Airs - November 28

Julie Andrews' first television special, "The Julie Andrews Show", aired on NBC and became an instant hit. It showcased her talents in singing, dancing, and hosting, with special appearances by Gene Kelly and The New Christy Minstrels. The special not only highlighted Andrews' remarkable versatility but also became a celebrated event in TV history. Viewers were charmed by Andrews' performance, with critics praising the show's lively entertainment and emotional warmth, solidifying her status as a beloved television and stage star.

Days of Our Lives

## Television Ratings 1965 (classic-tv.com)

### 1964-65 Shows

| Rank | Show | Estimated Audience |
| --- | --- | --- |
| 1 | Bonanza | 19,130,100 |
| 2 | Bewitched | 16,337,000 |
| 3 | Gomer Pyle, U.S.M.C. | 16,178,900 |
| 4 | The Andy Griffith Show | 14,914,100 |
| 5 | The Fugitive | 14,703,300 |
| 6 | The Red Skelton Show | 14,439,800 |
| 7 | The Dick Van Dyke Show | 14,281,700 |
| 8 | The Lucy Show | 14,018,200 |
| 9 | Peyton Place II | 13,912,800 |
| 10 | Combat | 13,754,700 |

## 1965-66 Shows

| Rank | Show | Estimated Audience |
| --- | --- | --- |
| 1 | Bonanza | 17,124,300 |
| 2 | Gomer Pyle, U.S.M.C. | 14,970,300 |
| 3 | The Lucy Show | 14,916,450 |
| 4 | The Red Skelton Show | 14,862,600 |
| 5 | Batman (Thursday) | 14,539,500 |
| 6 | The Andy Griffith Show | 14,485,650 |
| 7 | The Beverly Hillbillies | 13,947,150 |
| 8 | Hogan's Heroes | 13,408,650 |
| 9 | Batman (Wednesday) | 13,300,950 |
| 10 | Green Acres | 13,247,100 |

## The 22nd Golden Globe Awards – Monday, February 8th, 1965

### 🏆 Winners

In 1965, the Golden Globe Awards recognized only three categories:

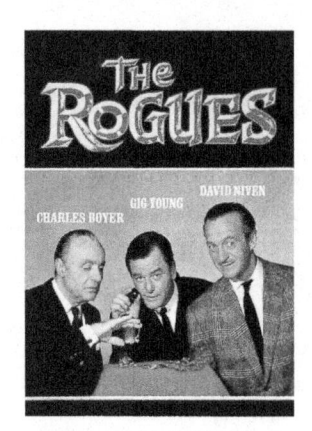

Best Television Series: The Rogues

Best TV Star - Male: Gene Barry (Burke's Law)

Best TV Star - Female: Mary Tyler Moore (The Dick Van Dyke Show)

# Chapter IV: Sports Review 1965

## American Sports

### NFL Championship Triumph: Packers Take the Title - December 27

The Packers' championship win at Lambeau Field was a mud-soaked, snowy battle that captivated over 50,000 fans braving frigid conditions. Green Bay,

*Packers QB Bart Starr prepares to hand off during NFL Championship vs. Browns*

led by the legendary Vince Lombardi and quarterback Bart Starr, outplayed the Cleveland Browns, whose star Jim Brown couldn't overcome a tough Packers defense. The game was the first NFL championship televised in color, adding to its significance. Despite the weather and a field that turned into a swamp, the Packers secured their ninth title with a 23-12 victory, marking the end of an era before the Super Bowl era would transform the league.

# 1965

## Fred Lorenzen: Daytona 500's Fastest - February 14

Fred Lorenzen

Fred Lorenzen's victory at Daytona came in a dramatic, rain-shortened race that saw fierce competition and plenty of chaos. Starting fourth, Lorenzen faced mechanical retirements, crashes, and tense moments, but edged past Marvin Panch just as rain began to fall. In a wild finish, Lorenzen's fender bent from contact, but his team gambled on the weather. As the skies opened, officials called the race after 133 laps, and Lorenzen was crowned champion. This was his first win of the season, cementing his status as one of NASCAR's elite in a race filled with speed, drama, and unexpected twists.

## Boston Celtics Conquer NBA Championship - April 18

The Boston Celtics clinched another NBA title in a dominant series against the Los Angeles Lakers, winning 4-1. With Elgin Baylor sidelined, the Lakers struggled to keep up with Bill Russell's incredible 25 rebounds per game and Sam Jones' scoring prowess. The Celtics averaged an impressive 123.4 points per game, outclassing the Lakers with ease. One of the most memorable moments came in Game 4 when, in a stunning turn

The Boston Celtics, World Champions of basketball, pose for a team portrait

of events, ABC cut away from the game during its final minutes. With this victory, Boston continued its reign as the NBA's powerhouse, further solidifying their dynasty in basketball history.

### King's Court: Manuel Santana's US Open Victory - September 12

Manuel Santana's stunning victory at the U.S. National Championships marked his rise to tennis greatness. Overcoming Cliff Drysdale in a thrilling four-set final, Santana showcased his skill and determination. Known for his witty remark that "grass is just for cows," he favored clay courts but proved his versatility with this hard-court triumph. His win, part of a breakout year where he also led Spain to a Davis Cup victory, cemented his status as a national hero. Santana's journey from a humble ball boy in Madrid to a world champion remains one of the most inspiring stories in tennis history.

Manuel Santana

### The Dodgers Secure MLB World Series Title: October 14

The Dodgers clinched the World Series title in a thrilling seven-game battle against the Minnesota Twins, with Sandy Koufax's legendary performance taking center stage.

The 1965 Dodgers

After missing Game 1 for Yom Kippur, Koufax lost Game 2 but rebounded to throw two masterful shutouts in Games 5 and 7. The Dodgers, reliant on their stellar pitching, turned the tide after losing the first two games. Willie Davis tied a World Series record with three stolen bases, and the Dodgers' dominance on the mound secured their victory. This triumph marked the team's second title in three years and solidified Koufax's place in baseball history.

## British Sports

### Liverpool Claims FA Cup - May 1

Liverpool secured their first-ever FA Cup victory in a thrilling match against Leeds United, finally breaking a long-standing curse in their third final appearance. Leeds, competing in their first final, were formidable opponents, but the match remained goalless after 90 minutes. In extra time, Roger Hunt gave Liverpool the lead, only for Leeds' Billy Bremner to quickly equalize. However, Ian St. John's header sealed the 2-1 win, sending Liverpool fans into a frenzy. This final also marked a historic moment, as Leeds' Albert Johanneson became the first black player to compete in an FA Cup final, enduring racial abuse but making a lasting impact on football history.

LFC's first FA Cup win in 1965. Queen Elizabeth II hands trophy to Captain Ron Yeats

## Stanley Matthews Retires - February 6

Sir Stanley Matthews, one of football's greatest icons, hung up his boots at the age of 50, ending a 35-year career that spanned generations. Known as "The Wizard of Dribble," Matthews dazzled fans with his extraordinary skill, longevity, and sportsmanship. He was the only player to be knighted while still playing and the first-ever Ballon d'Or winner. From his early days at Stoke City to his legendary FA Cup triumph with Blackpool, Matthews' influence extended beyond the pitch, as he coached and inspired players worldwide. His retirement marked the end of an era, leaving an indelible legacy in the world of football.

Sir Stanley Matthews

## West Ham United Triumphs: European Cup Winners' Cup - May 19

West Ham United triumphed in a thrilling European Cup Winners' Cup final, defeating 1860 Munich 2-0 at Wembley Stadium. After a tense, goalless first half, West Ham broke through in the 70th minute when Ronnie Boyce's pass found Alan Sealey, who scored from a tight angle. Just two minutes later, a free kick led to Bobby Moore's

West Ham United, 1965

cross, which Munich's goalkeeper failed to collect, allowing Sealey to score his second. The win, secured in front of nearly 98,000 fans, marked West Ham's first major European trophy, with captain Moore leading his side to a historic victory on home soil.

## Jay Trump Conquers: Grand National Champion - April 3

Jay Trump, an American thoroughbred with humble beginnings, made history by winning the prestigious English Grand National. After dominating the Maryland Hunt Cup twice, Jay Trump traveled to England, where he faced fierce competition. In a thrilling finish, he triumphed over Freddy, becoming the first American-owned, bred, and ridden horse to win the Grand National. His remarkable journey from unremarkable early races to steeplechase glory was guided by amateur jockey Tommy Smith. Jay Trump's legacy continued with a third Maryland Hunt Cup victory in 1966 before retirement, cementing his place as one of the greatest steeplechasers in history.

*Winner's circle celebration at Aintree after the 1965 Grand National*

## International Sports

### Gimondi Triumph: Tour de France Winner - July 14

In an astonishing debut, Felice Gimondi claimed victory in the Tour de France, becoming one of the few cyclists to win all three Grand Tours in

*Italy's Felice Gimondi at the 1965 Tour de France*

his career. Originally a substitute for his team, Gimondi quickly rose to the challenge, taking the lead in the third stage and defending it against seasoned riders like Raymond Poulidor. Despite Poulidor's fierce attacks on Mont Ventoux, Gimondi held his ground and even extended his lead in the mountain time trial. His performance on the final individual time trial sealed the win, making Gimondi's triumph one of the most remarkable in Tour de France history.

## Ali Conquers: Liston Rematch Victory - May 25

In one of boxing's most controversial showdowns, Muhammad Ali knocked out Sonny Liston in the first round of their rematch with a now-legendary "phantom punch." Many in the audience and even Ali himself seemed unsure whether the punch had landed, sparking decades of speculation about a possible fix. Ali's victory came amidst chaotic scenes, with the referee struggling to regain control as Ali stood over Liston, taunting him to get up. The fight, held in Lewiston, Maine, only deepened the

*Heavyweight champ Muhammad Ali stands over Sonny Liston after knockdown, Lewiston, Maine*

mystery surrounding Liston's fall, with accusations of mob involvement and conspiracy theories. Ali's emphatic win, though clouded by controversy, cemented his status as boxing's next great champion, while Liston's reputation never fully recovered.

## Nicklaus Dominates: Masters Golf Champion - April 11

*Nicklaus wins by nine to shatter Masters record*

Jack Nicklaus delivered a performance for the ages at the Masters, setting a new tournament record with a stunning score of 271, 17 under par. At just 25, Nicklaus overpowered Augusta National, leaving his rivals, including legends Arnold Palmer and Gary Player, far behind. His dominant third round of 64 tied the course record, showcasing his precision with short-irons and sheer power on the par fives. By the final round, Nicklaus sealed his victory by an incredible nine strokes—breaking the previous margin record and earning his second green jacket. Even Bobby Jones, Augusta's co-founder, marveled at Nicklaus' performance, famously remarking, "He plays a game with which I am not familiar."

## Emerson's Reign: Wimbledon Men's Singles Champion - July 2

Roy Emerson solidified his place in tennis history with a commanding victory at Wimbledon, defeating fellow Australian Fred Stolle in straight sets: 6–2, 6–4, 6–4. Defending his title with precision and finesse, Emerson

Roy Emerson

showcased his powerful baseline game and remarkable consistency throughout the tournament. This win marked Emerson's second Wimbledon singles crown, further establishing him as one of the premier players of his era. Despite Stolle's valiant effort, Emerson's dominance on the grass courts of the All England Club was undeniable, as he outplayed his opponent with superior shot selection and tactical brilliance, proving once again why he was the top seed of the tournament.

# Chapter V: General 1965

## Pop Culture

### The Beatles' Shea Stadium Concert: Rock Milestone - August 15

*Beatles concert at Shea Stadium*

The Beatles' concert at Shea Stadium marked a turning point in rock history, setting a new standard for stadium performances. With over 55,000 fans in attendance, it was the largest Beatles concert ever and the first major rock event of its kind. Amidst deafening screams and fan hysteria, the band delivered a set of classics like "Twist and Shout" and "Help!" Despite technical challenges and post-production tweaks, the energy and significance of the night were undeniable. The event became legendary, forever altering the landscape of live music performances.

### Rolling Stones' "Satisfaction" Becomes a Hit - July 10

The Rolling Stones' "Satisfaction" stormed the charts, cementing the band's place as rock icons. Featuring one of the most famous guitar riffs in music history,

*The Rolling Stones, 1965*

the song's raw energy and biting lyrics about commercialism and frustration resonated with listeners. It became the Stones' first number one hit in the US, despite initial controversy over its suggestive lyrics. Keith Richards famously wrote the iconic riff in his sleep, and its distinctive fuzz tone, paired with Mick Jagger's edgy vocals, helped make it a timeless anthem of rock rebellion.

## Bob Dylan Goes Electric at Newport Folk Festival - July 25

Bob Dylan's decision to go electric at the Newport Folk Festival shocked the folk community. With his amplified guitar and a full band, Dylan broke from tradition, performing "Maggie's Farm" and "Like a Rolling Stone" to a mix of cheers and boos. The performance divided fans, as some saw it as a bold move toward rock, while others felt betrayed by his shift from acoustic folk. Despite the controversy, this moment marked a pivotal turning point in music history, signaling the rise of folk rock and solidifying Dylan's legacy as an innovator.

Bob Dylan

## "Help!" Film and Album by The Beatles - August 6

The Beatles' "Help!" combined the release of a film and an album, showcasing the band's evolving sound. The album featured hits like "Help!" and "Ticket to Ride," along with "Yesterday," which became

Beatles released "Help" Album

the most covered song in history. It marked a creative shift for the Beatles, with richer instrumentation, including strings and flutes. Critics praised the album, which topped charts globally and earned the band their first Grammy nomination for Album of the Year. "Help!" is considered a significant moment in the Beatles' transition from pop sensations to serious musical innovators.

## "Dune" by Frank Herbert Published - August 1

"Dune", Frank Herbert's groundbreaking sci-fi novel, was first published by a company known for auto repair manuals, initially struggling to gain traction. Despite a slow start, word-of-mouth spread, and "Dune" grew into a monumental success, winning the Hugo and Nebula Awards. The novel explores themes of politics, religion, and ecology through the story of Paul Atreides and the coveted desert planet, Arrakis, home to the powerful "spice." "Dune" became one of the best-selling science fiction novels ever and inspired sequels, films, and even a mini-series, cementing its legendary status.

Dune

## Nat King Cole's Death - February 15

News of Nat King Cole's Death

Nat King Cole, the beloved singer and jazz pianist, passed away at the age of 45 after a battle with lung cancer. Known for timeless hits like "Unforgettable" and "Mona Lisa," Cole's smooth voice and groundbreaking achievements left an indelible mark on music. Despite facing racial barriers throughout his career, he became the first African American to host a national TV show. His final album, L-O-V-E, was recorded just months before his death, leaving behind a legacy that continues to inspire generations.

Nat King Cole

### Most Popular Books from 1965 (goodreads.com)

1. Dune (Dune, #1) - Frank Herbert
2. The Autobiography of Malcolm X - Malcolm X
3. Stoner - John Williams
4. Ariel - Sylvia Plath
5. The Mouse and the Motorcycle (Ralph S. Mouse, #1) - Beverly Cleary
6. The Magus - John Fowles
7. Fox in Socks - Dr. Seuss
8. Over Sea, Under Stone (The Dark is Rising, #1) - Susan Cooper
9. The Black Cauldron (The Chronicles of Prydain, #2) - Lloyd Alexander
10. The Source - James A. Michener
11. God Bless You, Mr. Rosewater - Kurt Vonnegut Jr.
12. The Three Stigmata of Palmer Eldritch - Philip K. Dick
13. The Painted Bird - Jerzy Kosiński
14. At Bertram's Hotel (Miss Marple, #11) - Agatha Christie

## Technological Advancements

### Gordon Moore Describes Moore's Law - April 19

Gordon Moore, co-founder of Intel, made a groundbreaking observation that the number of transistors in integrated circuits was doubling every year, predicting that this trend would continue. His prediction, now known as Moore's Law, became a

The Moore's Law

powerful force shaping the future of technology. It set a pace for exponential growth in computing power, leading to major advancements in electronics, from faster processors to more memory and better sensors. Although originally a bold prediction, Moore's Law has guided the semiconductor industry for decades, fueling innovation and driving economic growth worldwide.

### Kevlar Invented by Stephanie Kwolek at DuPont – 1965

Stephanie Kwolek's groundbreaking invention of Kevlar revolutionized materials science. While working at DuPont, she developed this incredibly strong, lightweight synthetic fiber, which is five times stronger than steel by weight.

DuPont textile fibers pioneering research laboratory

Initially created in search of a tire replacement, Kevlar's remarkable properties led to its use in over 200 applications, including bulletproof vests, ropes, airplanes, and building reinforcements. Kwolek's discovery not only impacted industries like aerospace and construction but also saved countless lives in law enforcement and the military. Her work earned her numerous accolades, including induction into the National Inventors Hall of Fame.

## Compact Disc Invented by James Russell – 1965

James Russell revolutionized the way we store and listen to music by inventing the concept of optical digital recording, which laid the foundation for the compact disc. Working at the Battelle Memorial Institute, he developed prototypes that used light to read and store data on discs, marking the early steps toward the CD format we know today. Although his early patents had limitations, Russell's innovative ideas about digital storage and playback were groundbreaking. His work was later built upon by companies like Philips and Sony, leading to the development of CDs that transformed the music industry.

James Russell

## First Portable Defibrillator Installed by Frank Pantridge - 1965

Frank Pantridge revolutionized emergency medicine with his invention of the portable defibrillator, making it possible to treat heart attacks on the spot rather than waiting for hospital care. His first model, powered by car batteries and installed in an ambulance, weighed 70 kilograms but soon evolved into a more portable 3-kg

Prof. Frank Pantridge with the original defibrillator

version. Despite initial skepticism in the UK, the device gained international recognition, saving countless lives, including that of U.S. President Lyndon Johnson. Pantridge's work laid the foundation for modern emergency medical protocols, earning him global acclaim as the "Father of Emergency Medicine."

## Gemini 6 & 7: First Space Rendezvous - December 15

In a landmark achievement, NASA's Gemini VI-A and Gemini VII completed the first-ever space rendezvous, a crucial step toward the Apollo Moon missions. Gemini VI-A, piloted by Wally Schirra and Tom Stafford, launched three days after technical issues delayed the mission. They successfully caught up with Gemini VII, commanded by Frank Borman and Jim Lovell, who were enduring a two-week endurance mission. For five hours, the two spacecraft maneuvered together, marking a triumph in space navigation. The missions paved the way for future space exploration, proving astronauts could rendezvous and survive extended spaceflight durations.

*Gemini 7 as seen from Gemini 6, during their rendezvous in space*

## PDP-8 Minicomputer Launched by Digital Equipment Corporation - March 22

Digital Equipment Corporation's PDP-8 transformed computing with its affordability and compact design, marking a significant leap in making computers accessible to smaller businesses and institutions. As the first commercially successful minicomputer, it combined simplicity, expandability,

# 1965

and low cost, which made it a favorite for many applications. Priced under $20,000, it quickly became the best-selling computer of its era. The PDP-8's 12-bit architecture and innovative design made programming more efficient, and its influence extended far beyond its time, laying the foundation for future advances in computing and helping shape the minicomputer industry.

A PDP-8 on display at The National Museum of Computing in Bletchley, England

## Fashion

Fashion in 1965 was a transformative moment, reflecting the cultural shifts of the decade. Youth-driven trends like the Mod movement brought bold experimentation, with women embracing miniskirts and A-line dresses, while men's fashion shifted towards slim-fit suits and modern tailoring. This era marked the rise of vibrant colors, new fabrics, and a rejection of conservative styles, setting the stage for fashion's evolution.

Women's fashion in 1965 was dominated by Mod influences and youth culture, bringing in a mix of playful and bold styles. The miniskirt, popularized by British designer Mary Quant, was the defining trend of the year. This daring, thigh-high skirt was often paired with go-go boots, creating an

Women's fashion in '65

Men's fashion in '65     Men's plaid pants

iconic look embraced by young women. Alongside the miniskirt, A-line dresses and shift dresses became wardrobe staples, featuring clean, geometric lines that echoed the modernist aesthetic of the era. These dresses came in bright colors or psychedelic patterns, reflecting the growing influence of art and pop culture.

Women's vibrant colors     The mini-Skirt in '65

# 1965

Mod style in '65

Go-go boots in the 60s

Plaid pants or sport coat with solid trousers

In terms of fabrics, rayon, cotton, and polyester blends were popular for their practicality and versatility. Dresses and skirts were often accompanied by bold prints, such as polka dots, checks, and florals. For outerwear, tailored coats and jackets were common, often made in tweeds or synthetic fabrics that gave structure without sacrificing comfort. Evening wear for women took a more glamorous turn, with velvet and satin dresses making appearances at formal events. These dresses were often designed with detachable collars and cuffs for versatility, while long, sleek lines maintained the elegant femininity of the time. Accessories like oversized

72

sunglasses, chunky jewelry, and wide belts were essential elements, enhancing both casual and formal looks.

Men's fashion in 1965 saw a shift towards a modern and tailored look, heavily influenced by European styles. The slim-fit suit was a key element of men's wardrobes, with jackets featuring slightly padded shoulders, natural waists, and slim trousers. These suits often came in muted colors like gray and olive, but plaid combinations and textured fabrics like hopsacking and corduroy also gained popularity.

Men's slim suits

Casual wear embraced denim and corduroy jackets, paired with turtlenecks and polo shirts. Men's pants varied from slim-tapered trousers to flared jeans, reflecting the growing interest in more relaxed, bohemian styles. Footwear was bold, with Chelsea boots and Cuban heels becoming popular. Accessories like fedoras, slim ties, and dark sunglasses completed the Mod

Mick Jagger in a turtleneck sweater while rehearsing

# 1965

*Jimi Hendrix in Chelsea boots*

and preppy looks of the time, giving men's fashion an edge that balanced sophistication with youthful rebellion.

In essence, fashion in 1965 reflected a blend of youth-driven experimentation for women and a refined yet modern look for men, cementing the year as a cornerstone of mid-century style.

## Cars

The car industry in 1965 was thriving, fueled by an economic boom and consumer enthusiasm for stylish, powerful cars. This year saw the rise of iconic models, particularly muscle cars and compact family vehicles. With manufacturers pushing the boundaries of performance and design, 1965 became a memorable year in automotive history, particularly in the U.S. and U.K., where distinct preferences shaped the market.

### Top Selling Cars

*1965 Chevrolet Impala*

#### U.S.A.

In 1965, the Chevrolet Impala dominated the American market, with over 1 million units sold, making it one of the best-selling cars of all time. Known for its sleek design and powerful engine options, the Impala appealed to a wide range of buyers, from families to enthusiasts. Its continued success solidified Chevrolet's position as a leader in the American auto industry during the 1960s.

Another standout was the Ford Mustang, which had been introduced in 1964. By 1965, the Mustang was already a cultural phenomenon, with 559,451 units sold. Its sporty design, coupled with its affordability, made it the perfect car for young drivers and set the stage for the muscle car era to flourish.

1965 Ford Mustang

## U.K.

1965 Ford Cortina

In the U.K., the best-selling car of 1965 was the Ford Cortina, which maintained its dominance in the British market. Over 126,000 units were sold that year, a testament to its blend of reliability, affordability, and style. The Cortina offered a wide variety of models and trims, allowing it to appeal to different segments of the population. Closely following the Cortina was the Mini, with its compact size and excellent fuel efficiency. The Mini was a symbol of British ingenuity and design, and its popularity grew steadily throughout the 1960s. In 1965, it continued to capture the imagination of both city drivers and racing enthusiasts.

1965 Mini

## Fastest Car

In 1965, the title for the fastest car went to the Shelby Cobra 427. This American icon, powered by a 7.0-liter V8 engine, produced 425 horsepower and could hit a top speed of 164 mph. The Cobra's stunning performance made it a favorite among car enthusiasts, and its aggressive design helped it stand out in the burgeoning muscle car market.

1965 Shelby Cobra 427

## Most Expensive American Car of 1965

1965 Cadillac Eldorado

The Cadillac Eldorado was the most expensive American car in 1965, with a base price of around $6,600. Known for its luxury and sophisticated design, the Eldorado featured a powerful V8 engine, plush interiors, and advanced technology for its time, such as automatic climate control. The car was a symbol of status and opulence, appealing to affluent buyers seeking both performance and comfort.

## Most Powerful Muscle Car of 1965

1965 Pontiac GTO

The Pontiac GTO stood as the most powerful muscle car of 1965. Equipped with an optional 389 cubic inch V8 engine producing up to 360 horsepower, the GTO could go from 0 to 60 mph in under six seconds. This performance, combined with its aggressive styling and affordability, earned it the nickname "The Goat" and made it one of the most iconic muscle cars of the decade.

1965 was a landmark year for the automotive industry, marked by innovation and fierce competition. Whether it was the family-friendly Impala, the stylish Mustang, or the roaring Shelby Cobra, car manufacturers delivered models that would leave a lasting impact on automotive history. In both the U.S. and U.K., consumers had more options than ever before, each catering to their specific desires for speed, style, or practicality.

## Popular Recreation

In 1965, the energy of post-war optimism blended with the advent of new technologies and cultural shifts, creating a dynamic range of recreational and leisure activities for both young and old. From the rise of TV shows to outdoor hobbies and family games, the year reflected the burgeoning influence of

# 1965

youth culture and the evolving role of technology in everyday life.

Music was at the heart of popular recreation in 1965. The British Invasion—led by bands like The Beatles and The Rolling Stones—swept across the U.S., influencing not only what people listened to but how they spent their free time. Teenagers gathered at parties or local dance halls to twist, shimmy, and groove to hits like "I Can't Get No Satisfaction." Live music venues thrived, particularly in urban centers like London and New York, where rock and roll acts performed nightly. Dancing remained a popular pastime, with new dances such as the Frug and Watusi rising in popularity, particularly among young people.

Teenagers dancing the Watusi at Hollywood nightclub

At the same time, jazz clubs were packed with patrons drawn to the evolving sounds of artists like John Coltrane and Miles Davis, while folk music found a devoted following among those seeking more politically conscious entertainment. In coffeehouses and smaller

John Coltrane and his quartet played a set at Seattle's Penthouse Jazz Club

Folk musicians gathering in Washington Square ParkPenthouse Jazz Club

venues, fans gathered to hear Bob Dylan, Joan Baez, and other folk icons sing about civil rights and war.

Board games were a staple in households in both the U.S. and the U.K. in 1965, with classics like Monopoly and Scrabble dominating family game

1965 Cluedo board set

Family playing Monopoly

nights. However, one game that caught the imagination of many in the U.K. was Cluedo (known as Clue in the U.S.), where players tested their detective skills by solving fictional murders.

A game of Scrabble in progress

1965 Crown Firecoach Engine 51 "Los Angeles County Fire Dept."

Group of men playing the slot car racing

For indoor hobbies, model building became a favored pastime, particularly with boys and young men. They meticulously constructed scale models of cars, planes, and rockets, influenced by the ongoing Space Race between the U.S. and the Soviet Union. Slot-car racing, which saw its "golden age" in the mid-1960s, captured the attention of hobbyists who constructed elaborate tracks at home.

Television was another major player in leisure activities. In the U.S., families gathered around the TV to watch popular sitcoms such as "Gilligan's Island" and "The Munsters", as well as Westerns like "Bonanza". In the U.K., shows

The cast of "Gilligan's Island"

like "Doctor Who" and "Coronation Street" became cultural phenomena, and watching TV became a collective ritual, with limited channels creating a shared viewing experience for all ages.

"The Bonanza" full cast

The cast of "The Munsters"

Doctor Who

Sports were central to recreation in 1965. Baseball remained America's favorite pastime, with families flocking to local games or watching major league broadcasts. Bowling, too, continued its rise in popularity, with millions of Americans participating in leagues across the country. Meanwhile, in the U.K., football (soccer) captured the public's attention, with teams like Manchester United and Liverpool drawing thousands to their matches.

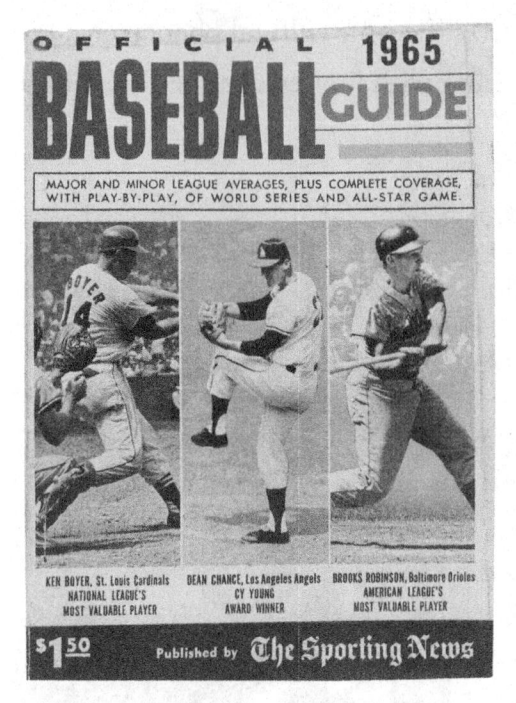

# 1965

The Sporting News Issue in 1965 with the Baseball Guide as one of the sections

Bowling in 1965

Three people fishing from a boat, having fun in 1965

Outdoor hobbies flourished, with fishing and cycling proving popular across both continents. Surfing on the West Coast of the U.S. and skateboarding—a newer trend—were especially popular with younger generations. The sport of golf also experienced a resurgence, attracting both casual players and those drawn to televised tournaments, such as the Masters.

For younger children, toys like Troll dolls and GI Joe action figures became must-haves. Troll dolls, with their brightly colored hair, captured the hearts of young girls, while boys collected and played with their GI Joe figurines,

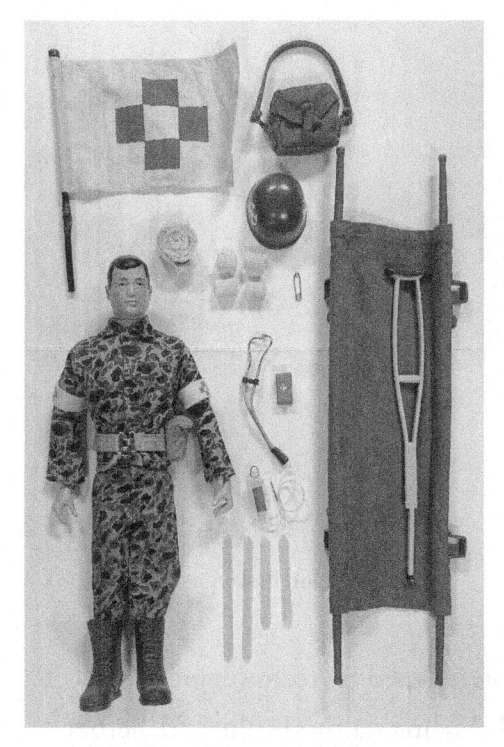

1965

1965 Hasbro 12" G.I. Joe Marine medic figure & equipment set

Troll dolls

Sindy with her frosty night outfits

Meccano set

imagining military adventures. The popularity of Legos, first introduced in the late 1950s, continued to grow as new sets were introduced, allowing children to build complex structures and fuel their imaginations.

In the U.K., toys like Meccano sets and Hornby train sets entertained boys, while girls often enjoyed dolls like Sindy—the British counterpart to

83

Hornby train set

Barbie. Marble games and jacks were also popular, providing simple, engaging fun.

Children playing marbles

By 1965, recreation and leisure activities were becoming more varied and accessible, shaped by technological advancements, the rise of television, and shifting cultural values. Whether gathering around the TV for family shows, dancing to the latest hits, or building model rockets, people across the U.S. and U.K. found new ways to entertain themselves, reflecting the growing spirit of innovation and fun that defined the decade.

# Chapter VI: Births & Deaths 1965

## Births (onthisday.com)

January 22nd – Diane Lane: American Actress

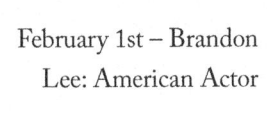

February 1st – Brandon Lee: American Actor

February 11th – Varg Vikernes: Norwegian Musician

February 12th – Brett Kavanaugh: American Supreme Court Justice

February 17th – Michael Bay: American Film Director

February 18th – Dr. Dre: American Rapper and Music Producer

March 25th – Sarah Jessica Parker: American Actress

March 30th – Piers Morgan: British TV Show Host

April 2nd – Rodney King: American Civil Rights Figure

April 4th – Robert Downey Jr.: American Actor

April 16th – Martin Lawrence: American Actor and Comedian

April 19th – Suge Knight: American Music Producer

# 1965

April 24th – Cedric the Entertainer: American Comedian

May 10th – Linda Evangelista: Canadian Supermodel

May 17th – Trent Reznor: American Musician

May 24th – John C. Reilly: American Actor

June 10th – Elizabeth Hurley: British Actress and Model

July 22nd – Shawn Michaels: American Professional Wrestler

July 23rd – Slash: British-American Guitarist

July 26th – Jeremy Piven: American Actor

August 1st – Sam Mendes: British Film Director

August 11th – Viola Davis: American Actress

August 19th – Kyra Sedgwick: American Actress

August 20th – KRS-One: American Rapper

August 28th – Shania Twain: Canadian Country Singer

September 3rd – Charlie Sheen: American Actor

September 11th – Moby: American Musician

September 14th – Dmitry Medvedev: Russian Politician, former President and Prime Minister

September 25th – Scottie Pippen: American Basketball Player

October 1st – Michaele Salahi: American Reality Star

October 18th – Erin Moran: American Actress

November 21st – Björk: Icelandic Singer

November 30th – Ryan Murphy: American TV Producer

December 3rd – Katarina Witt: German Figure Skater

December 21st – Andy Dick: American Comedian and Actor

December 31st – Gong Li: Chinese Actress

## Deaths (onthisday.com)

January 14th – Jeanette MacDonald: American Movie Actress

January 20th – Alan Freed: American DJ

February 21st – Malcolm X: American Civil Rights Leader

February 22nd – Felix Frankfurter: American Supreme Court Justice

February 23rd – Stan Laurel: British-American Comedian and Actor

April 27th – Edward R. Murrow: American Journalist

# 1965

May 1st – Spike Jones: American Comedian and Musician

May 14th – Frances Perkins: American Politician

May 24th – Sonny Boy Williamson II: American Blues Musician

June 13th – Martin Buber: Austrian Philosopher

June 22nd – David O. Selznick: American Film Producer

July 14th – Adlai Stevenson II: American Politician

July 19th – Syngman Rhee: South Korean President

August 31st – E. E. Smith: American Science Fiction Writer

September 4th – Albert Schweitzer: Franco-German Theologian and Physician

November 2nd – H. V. Evatt: Australian Politician

November 6th – Edgard Varèse: French-American Composer

November 16th – W. T. Cosgrave: Irish Political Leader

November 18th – Henry A. Wallace: American Vice President

December 9th – Branch Rickey: American Baseball Executive

December 10th – Henry Cowell: American Composer

December 16th – W. Somerset Maugham: British Writer

# **Chapter VII:** Statistics 1965

## GDP

- ✸ U.S. GDP 1965 – 741.90 billion USD (worldbank.org)
- ✸ U.S. GDP 2023 – 27.36 trillion USD (worldbank.org)
- ✸ U.K. GDP 1965 – 181.82 billion USD (worldbank.org)
- ✸ U.K. GDP 2023 – 3.34 trillion USD (worldbank.org)

## Inflation

- ✸ U.S. Inflation 1965 – 1.6% (worldbank.org)
- ✸ U.S. Inflation 2023 – 4.1% (worldbank.org)
- ✸ U.K. Inflation 1965 – 4.8% (worldbank.org)
- ✸ U.K. Inflation 2023 – 6.8% (worldbank.org)

## Population

- ✸ U.S. Population 1965 – 194,303,000 (worldbank.org)
- ✸ U.S. Population 2023 - 334,914,895 (worldbank.org)
- ✸ U.K. Population 1965 – 54,348,050 (worldbank.org)
- ✸ U.K. Population 2023 - 68,350,000 (worldbank.org)

## Life Expectancy at Birth

- ✸ U.S. Life Expectancy at Birth 1965 - 70 (worldbank.org)
- ✸ U.S. Life Expectancy at Birth 2022 – 77 (worldbank.org)
- ✸ U.K. Life Expectancy at Birth 1965 – 72 (worldbank.org)
- ✸ U.K. Life Expectancy at Birth 2022 – 82 (worldbank.org)

## Annual Working Hours Per Worker

- ✸ U.S. Annual Working Hours Per Worker 1965 - 1,953 (ourworldindata.org)

* U.S. Annual Working Hours Per Worker 2017 - 1,657 (ourworldindata.org)
* U.K. Annual Working Hours Per Worker 1965 - 1,998 (ourworldindata.org)
* U.K. Annual Working Hours Per Worker 2017 - 1,670 (ourworldindata.org)

## Unemployment Rate

* U.S. Unemployment Rate 1965 – 4.0% (thebalancemoney.com)
* U.S. Unemployment Rate 2023 – 3.6% (worldbank.org)
* U.K. Unemployment Rate 1965 - 1.7% (fullfact.org)
* U.K. Unemployment Rate 2023 – 4.0% (ons.gov.uk)

## Tax Revenue (% of GDP)

* U.S. Tax Revenue (% of GDP) 1965 – 27.73% (imf.org)
* U.S. Tax Revenue (% of GDP) 2022 – 12.2% (worldbank.org)
* U.K. Tax Revenue (% of GDP) 1965 – 32.51% (imf.org)
* U.K. Tax Revenue (% of GDP) 2022 – 27.3% (worldbank.org)

## Prison Population

* U.S. Prison Population 1965 - 210,895 (bjs.ojp.gov)
* U.S. Prison Population 2021 - 1,230,100 (bjs.ojp.gov)
* U.K. Prison Population 1965 - 37,000 (parliament.uk)
* U.K. Prison Population 2023 - 97,700 (parliament.uk)

## Average Cost of a New House

* U.S. Average Cost of a New House 1965 – $21,500 (census.gov)
* U.S. Average Cost of a New House 2023 – $495,100 (dqydj.com)
* U.K. Average Cost of a New House 1965 – £3,360 (ons.gov.uk)
* U.K. Average Cost of a New House 2023 – £290,000 (ons.gov.uk)

## Average Income per Year

- U.S. Average Income per Year 1965 – $6,450 (bea.gov)
- U.S. Average Income per Year US 2023 – $106,400 (multpl.com)
- U.K. Average Income per Year 1965 – £3,000 (bjs.ojp.gov)
- U.K. Average Income per Year 2023 – £34,963 (statista.com)

## U.S. Cost of Living

The $100 from 1965 has grown to about $1,000.96 today, up $900.96 over 59 years due to an average yearly inflation of 3.98%, resulting in a 900.96% total price hike (in2013dollars.com).

## U.K. Cost of Living

Today's £2,426.60 mirrors the purchasing power of £100 in 1965, showing a £2,326.60 hike over 59 years. The pound's yearly inflation rate averaged 5.55% during this period, leading to a 2,326.60% total price rise (in2013dollars.com).

## Cost Of Things

### United States

- Men's raincoats: $15.00 - $24.95 (mclib.info)
- Men's shirts, Arrow: $4.00 (mclib.info)
- Women's suit, 3 piece bonded knit: $7.96 (mclib.info)
- Fresh eggs (1 dozen): $0.53 (stacker.com)
- White bread (1 pound): $0.21 (stacker.com)
- Sliced bacon (1 pound): $0.69 (mclib.info)
- Round steak (1 pound): $1.08 (stacker.com)
- Potatoes (10 pounds): $0.79 (mclib.info)
- Fresh delivered milk (1/2 gallon): $0.53 (stacker.com)

- ★ Coffee, Nescafe, instant (1 lb can): $1.50 (mclib.info)
- ★ Apples, Red Delicious (3 lbs): $0.19 (mclib.info)
- ★ Butter, Land O'Lakes (1 lb): $0.69 (mclib.info)
- ★ Beef, ground chuck (1 pound): $0.59 (mclib.info)
- ★ Beans, baked, Van Camp's (1 lb can): $1.00 for 10 cans (mclib.info)
- ★ Soup, Campbell's (6 cans): $1.00 (mclib.info)
- ★ Ketchup, Heinz (14 oz bottle): $1.00 for 5 bottles (mclib.info)

**United Kingdom (retrowow.co.uk)**

- ★ Gallon of petrol: 6s 2d
- ★ Half a bottle of Scotch whisky: £1 1s 9d to £1 5s 3d
- ★ Pint of beer: 2s 4d
- ★ 20 cigarettes: 4s 7d
- ★ Pint of milk: 9½d
- ★ Large loaf of bread: 1s 2½d
- ★ 11" Ferguson black & white TV: £59 17s
- ★ 19" black & white TV rental (per week): 8s 6d to 11s
- ★ Decca TP99 radio: £15 15s
- ★ Ferguson reel-to-reel tape recorder: £25 4s
- ★ Olympus Pen-EE camera: £28 7s
- ★ The Daily Mirror newspaper: 4d
- ★ Pepsi Cola (can): 10½d
- ★ Ford Cortina car: £644
- ★ Hotpoint Iced Diamond refrigerator: £65 2s
- ★ A dozen eggs: 3s 8d to 4s 6d

# Chapter VIII: Iconic Advertisements of 1965

Pan Am Airlines

Converse

Sony: Anyplace Sony Tv

Budweiser

1965

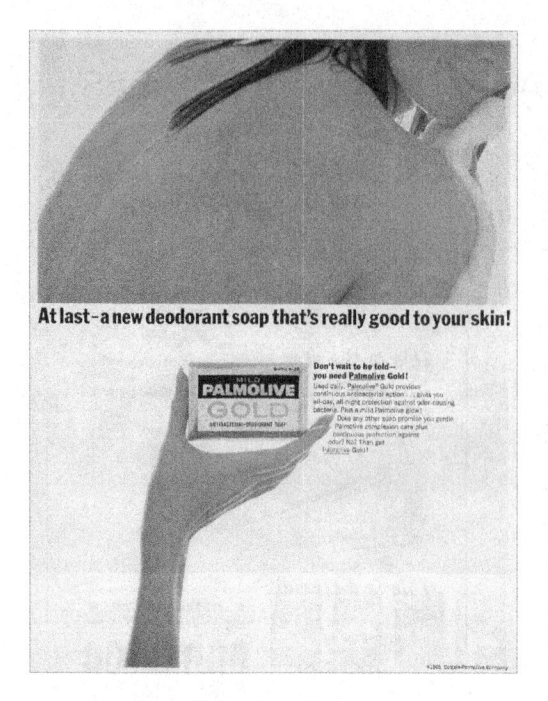

Palmolive Gold

Bell System

Gordon's Gin

Campbell's Soup

1965

Camel

Coppertone

Philips: Transistors

Jim Beam

1965

Quaker Oats: Diet Frosted

Chesterfield King

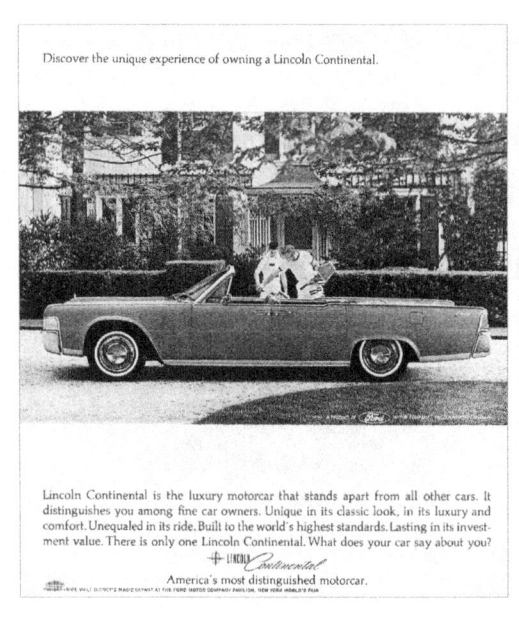

Lincoln Continental '65

Pepsi-Cola

1965

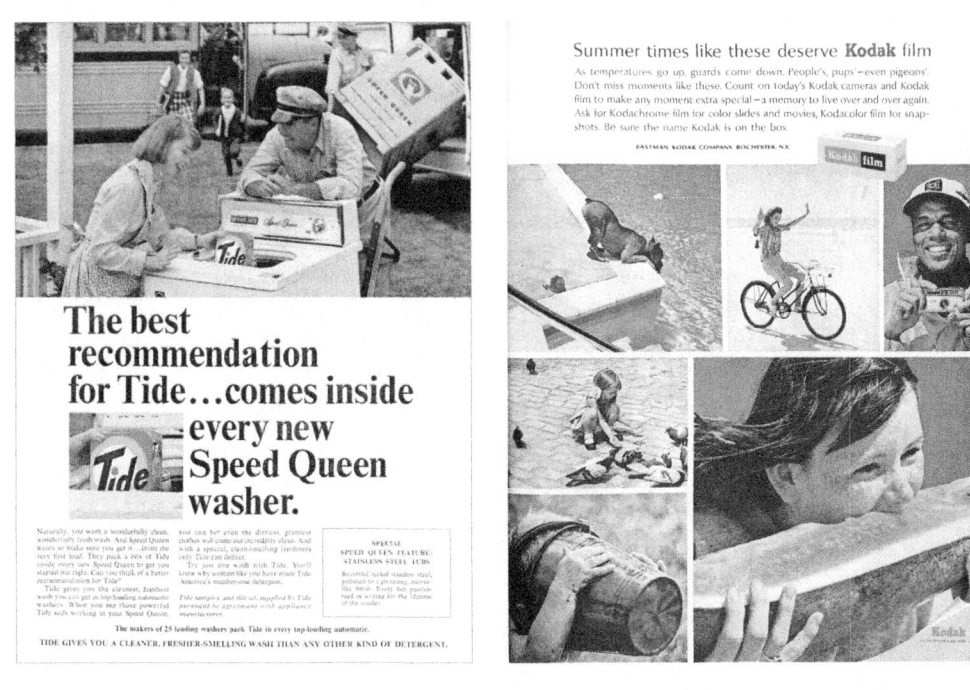

Tide

Kodak Film

Smirnoff Vodka

McDonald's

97

1965

Marlboro: Roosevelt Brown, All Pro Tackle, New York Football Giants

Chevrolet Impala '65

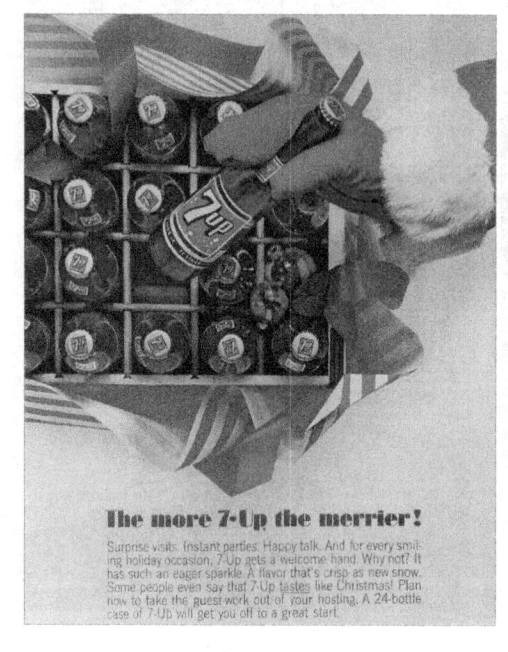

7-Up

Firestone

1965

General Electric: Color Television

Jose Cuervo Tequila

Kellogg's: Corn Flakes

Lucky Strike

1965

Pontiac Bonneville '65

Coca-Cola

## I have a gift for you!

Dear reader, thank you so much for reading my book!

To make this book more (much more!) affordable, all images are in black and white, but I've created a special gift for you!

You can now have access, for FREE, to the PDF version of this book with the original images!

Keep in mind that some are originally black and white, but some are colored.

I hope you enjoy it!

Download it here:

bit.ly/418BOBN

*Or* Scan this QR Code:

## I have a favor to ask you!

I deeply hope you've enjoyed reading this book and felt transported right into 1965!

I loved researching it, organizing it, and writing it, knowing that it would make your day a little brighter.

If you've enjoyed it too, I would be extremely grateful if you took just a few minutes to leave a positive customer review and share it with your friends.

As an unknown author, that makes all the difference and gives me the extra energy I need to keep researching, writing, and bringing joy to all my readers. Thank you!

*Best regards,*
*Owen J. Wilder*

Please leave a positive book review here:

https://amzn.to/3Vc9qeq

*Or* Scan this QR Code:

# Discover Other Books in this Collection!

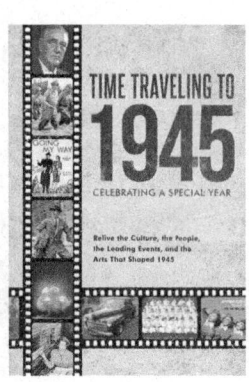

Made in the USA
Coppell, TX
22 May 2025

49690519R00059